THE LEWIS AND CLARK EXPEDITION:

A HISTORY JUST FOR KIDS

BRIAN ROGERS

KidLit-O Books
ANAHEIM, CALIFORNIA

Copyright © 2019 by Golgotha Press, Inc.

All rights reserved. No part of this publication may be reproduced, distributed or transmitted in any form or by any means, including photocopying, recording, or other electronic or mechanical methods, without the prior written permission of the publisher, except in the case of brief quotations embodied in critical reviews and certain other noncommercial uses permitted by copyright law.

Contents

About KidLit-O 1

Introduction 3

What led up to Lewis and Clark's journey? 10

Why did Lewis and Clark make their journey? 19

What happened during Lewis and Clark's adventure? 23

What was it like to be a kid travelling with Lewis and Clark? 35

How did Lewis and Clark's journey end? 38

    What happened after Lewis and Clark completed their journey? 39

Conclusion 44

About KidLit-O

KidLit-O is an imprint of BookCaps™ that is just for kids! Each month BookCaps will be releasing several books in this exciting imprint. Visit our website or like us on Facebook to see more!
To add your name to our mailing list, visit this link: http://www.kidlito.com/mailing-list.html

2 | The Lewis and Clark Expedition

[1]
Introduction

It was a beautiful spring day on April 29, 1805. Meriwether Lewis was exploring the area around the Missouri River, the first time that any white man had explored so far west on the majestic river. With a handful of men, he was trying to get to see all the new types of wildlife that were unknown at the time to Americans living in the Eastern United States.

Before crossing the Rocky Mountain Range, Lewis, as leader of the expedition, was looking for a good place to stay for the winter. He knew how dangerous it would be to travel with his group, including horses and canoes, on a frozen river and in deep snow. So, when the group met the Native American tribe called the Mandan, they decided to build a shelter for the winter nearby, and called it "Fort Mandan."

All during the winter, they traded with the Mandan people, they made clothes to keep themselves warm, and they spoke with their neighbors about what they might find on the other side of the Rocky Mountain Range (called "the Continental Divide". The Mandan told them of many exciting things, but Lewis thought that they might be exaggerating a little bit. For example, they told him of a creature so large that it can kill a man with just one hit, and that it runs very quickly and is very difficult to kill. Lewis thought that this creature, if it even was real, was probably intimidating to the Native Americans because they only had bows and arrows. His men, however, had guns. Surely, there was no way that such a creature could cause them any trouble.

On April 29, 1805, Meriwether Lewis and his men were not thinking about what the Mandan people had told them. They were focused on looking at smaller animals and some local plants. Imagine their surprise when they looked up and saw two huge grizzly bears running towards them. Have you ever seen a grizzly bear before? Do you know how big they can get?

An adult male grizzly bear can weigh about 800 pounds, although some have been found that weight over 1,200 pounds (the same as a small car).

When they stand on their hind legs, they can be from seven to ten feet tall! Lewis and his men were so surprised that they just started running. They shot and wounded one of the bears (who escaped) and then they were chased for almost 250 feet by the other, before they were able to shoot and kill it. What do you think: did Lewis finally believe the Native Americans when they told him about dangerous animals? Did he start listening more when they warned him of other dangerous plants and animals?

Up to that point, Lewis and his men hadn't been scared of the bears, just curious. Later on, after a few more encounters like the one we just read about, Lewis wrote in his journal: "I find the curiosity of our men with respect to this animal is pretty much satisfied." In other words, they didn't want to see any more bears. They could spend the rest of their journey without seeing a bear, and Lewis would be okay with that.

Surviving the grizzly attack was just one of many adventures that Meriwether Lewis would have on his journey across the United States. Together with his partner, William Clark, he would face hostile Native Americans, bitterly cold winters, fierce animals, wild rivers, and lonely fur trappers. They would see things that had never before seen by white American eyes, and they would bring a whole new world of flora and fauna (plants and animals) to the attention of the President of the United States (Thomas Jefferson). They were going to have a real American adventure.

What do you know about Meriwether Lewis and William Clark? Do you know where they came from, and who asked them to cross the country? Do you know why they were so happy to do it? Do you know what they actually expected to find in their journey?

Meriwether Lewis was born in Virginia on August 18, 1774, and William Clark was born on August 1, 1770, also in Virginia. Both men later joined the army, and Lewis came to have the rank of Captain. For a time, he served under Clark. The two men knew each other well. Lewis had also known President Thomas Jefferson from when they were back in Virginia, and so when Jefferson was elected President, Lewis became his aide, even living with him in the mansion and speaking with a lot of famous politicians that came to visit.

In the early 1800s, most Americans were focused on living their lives east of the Continental Divide. There were large plantations, companies, shipping businesses, and so on, but there was always the big question: what's beyond the land that we have seen so far? In particular, President Thomas Jefferson wanted to know if there was a way to travel by water from one coast to the other. He knew that two rivers flowed from the same general area: the Missouri River and the Columbia River, one to the east and one to the west. If it was possible to take some ships up one river and down the other, then the American merchants could sail right to Asia with hardly any problems. They could make lots of money trading and selling with new clients.

What's more, there was an intense scientific interest in knowing more about the plants, animals, and Native American tribes that lived on the other side of the Continental Divide. Lewis and Clark were to be explorers, ambassadors, and investigators all at the same time. They were going to try to find the Northwest Passage (a way to cross the United States by water) and they were going to explore the new lands, and write about the species and peoples that they saw along the way. However, as we will see, there were also some political reasons behind their trip also.

So, what will we be looking at in this report? First, we will learn a little bit more about the history of exploration in the United States, and of some of the people who made dangerous journeys before Lewis and Clark went on theirs. Then, we will learn about some of the specific reasons that President Thomas Jefferson sent Lewis on Clark on their journey. After that, we will go along with Lewis and Clark on their journey and have some adventures with them. We will meet some hostile Sioux Native Americans, we will run from Grizzly bears, and we will try not to drown in the icy rivers as we go down them quickly in our little canoes.

We will also talk about what it was like to be a kid in those days, and what a kid would have felt like traveling with Lewis and Clark. Then, we will see how the journey finally came to an end, and what happened after.

Are you ready to learn about all this? Then keep reading and we will set sail with Lewis and Clark, real American adventurers!

[2] What led up to Lewis and Clark's journey?

Lewis and Clark were not the first men sent out to explore the Western part of the United States. For almost three hundred years, one explorer after another would try to see what riches were there, what the Native American tribes were like, and whether or not it was dangerous. Along with a spirit of adventure, there was also the promise of money. For example, some explorers were traders who looked for new people to trade with. Others were fur trappers who wanted to finds new animals to hunt. Others were looking for mythical places (like the Fountain of Youth). While each one had his motivation, these explorers helped to pave the way for those who would follow.

Let's see a few of the more noteworthy examples.

Back in 1537, Álvar Núñez Cabeza de Vaca (an explorer from Spain) wanted to learn a little more about the New World that Spain was so interested in. Spain had mostly focused its attention on South America and the Caribbean Islands, but they were also curious if there was any money to be made in the Northern part of the New World. With the goal of exploring the Northern part further, 600 men were sent out from Spain to explore the Gulf of Mexico. Only four survived.

Álvar Núñez Cabeza de Vaca was a ranking officer in the group, but the leader was a man named Pánfilo de Narváez. After stopping at Cuba and Hispaniola for supplies, they got near the mouth of the Mississippi River, where a hurricane destroyed some of the ships (some were lost forever, including the leader's). The rest of the men landed ashore, and were enslaved by local Native Americans. They didn't have enough food, they got sick, and they were treated badly by their masters. After three years, only four men were still alive, including Cabeza de Vaca. The four escaped, and made their way to Mexico City. Afterwards, they explored what is known today as Texas and the American Southwest. They later returned to Spain, and made records of their journeys. These records would excite and help future explorers.

In 1540–42 Francisco Vásquez de Coronado (another Spanish explorer) journeyed from Arizona to eastern Kansas. He had hoped to find great riches in the New World, especially in the mythical "Seven Cities of Gold" (which, or course, didn't exist). He pushed northward with a large group of men. They faced bad storms and starvation. The local Native Americans didn't want to help them, and there were even a few battles. By the time they got as far north as Kansas, Coronado realized that there were probably no cities full of gold, and he decided to stop searching. Right about then, he also had a nasty fall from his horse, and his men persuaded him to go home.

About the same time, Hernando de Soto was exploring the Southern United States. He also had problems with Native Americans, even attacking and destroying one of their larger villages. He did not find any riches or worthwhile investments either.

Because these first three expeditions into the New World had failed to make any money, Spain decided that it really wasn't worth their time to explore any more. From that point on, most of the explorers were either privately funded (meaning they got the money for their trip from companies and investors) or were from other countries.

For example, in 1682, the French (who had established the territory of Quebec in Canada) sent René-Robert Cavelier from the Great Lakes region all the way down the Mississippi to the Gulf of Mexico. After his trip, the French (who were getting a lot of money by trading with Native Americans) set up a lot of trading post along the river. A later French explorer, named Etiene Veniard, went up the Missouri River to explore that region also.

In the late 1600s, a Native American named Moncacht-Apé travelled all the way from the Atlantic Ocean to the Pacific Ocean. He later told a French writer about his travels. Lewis and Clark actually carried a copy of this report with them, and used it when looking for the Northwest Passage. However, there was one detail that Moncacht-Apé neglected to mention in his report: the existence of the Rocky Mountain Range. Because the report only mentioned sailing up one river and down the other, some who read the report (including President Thomas Jefferson) thought that it would be an easy thing to take a boat from one side of the country to the other. Of course, Lewis and Clark would put this theory to the test during their journey.

Meanwhile, ships that had travelled around the southern tip of South America (Cape Horn) of the southern tip of Africa (Cape Agulhas) were able to find their way past Hawaii all the way to the West Coast of the United States. For example, in 1778, James Cook (a British explorer) decided to explore the Pacific Coast. As the British decided to expand more and more, they began to start fur trading with China, and even had some run-ins with local Native American tribes.

In 1792, there was an official group put together in London called the Vancouver Expedition. During their long journey in the Pacific Ocean, they sailed right into the Columbia River (modern day Washington and Oregon) and went up it as far as they could. The map that they made was later used by Lewis and Clark as they tried to find their way down the river towards the Pacific.

As we can see, there was a lot of excitement about the land that was in between the Mississippi River and the Pacific Ocean. No one had really been able to walk through it and write down what they saw. No one knew what ways there were to make money, of if people could even live there. Back then, when there were no satellites in the skies and no airplanes, the only way to learn about a new place was to go there and explore it personally.

But how could they arrange such a complicated mission? In order to be successful, it would be necessary to have the best explorers, the most reliable maps and guides, special training, and the necessary funding (money). Really, the only way that all of that could happen would be if the President of the Unites States approved it!

And that is exactly what happened. One man who helped to make all of that possible was John Ledyard. Who was John Ledyard?

John Ledyard was a British citizen born in Connecticut in 1751, before the American Revolution. He sailed with Captain James Cook on his third voyage in 1778, when the Pacific Northwest was explored. He saw how much money was to be made trading furs with China. Knowing that there were a lot of furs in the unexplored regions of the United States West of the Mississippi, Ledyard eventually met Thomas Jefferson in the 1780s, when Jefferson was still just an American Ambassador. He got Jefferson so excited about the prospects of exploring and taking advantage of these new lands that Jefferson, together with other important figures of the time, gave Ledyard enough money to travel to Russia and to try to cross the Bering Strait over to Alaska and down to the Western United States that way.

Although John Ledyard wasn't successful, a fire had been lit in Thomas Jefferson's soul. He was convinced that it was America's Destiny to push westward all the way to the Pacific Ocean. He would have his chance to see his dream of exploring the West come true soon enough. With the success of the Louisiana Purchase (which we will discuss a little later) Congress finally approved the formation of a new branch of the military, called the Discovery Corps, in order to explore the West.

What kind of people would be needed to do a job like that? As we saw, Lewis and Clark were both former soldiers, and had a lot of experience living in tough conditions. They had fought in wars and had learned how to live out of tents and hunt for their food. However, more would be needed, especially because the U.S. Government wanted to see some scientific research done along the way. Meriwether Lewis was perfect for the job.

Lewis loved to go out at night to hunt. His mother taught him how to gather natural herbs from the forest, and he became quite the outdoorsman. When he left home at the age of thirteen, he had already been told by some people that he should be a traveler or an explorer. In 1801, he was appointed as aide to President Jefferson, and then was chosen to be the leader on the expedition a few years later. He even bought a huge Newfoundland dog named Seaman, who would accompany them on the entire trip.

Even though Lewis was very comfortable being in the outdoors, the government wanted to make sure that he got the absolute best training possible. With that in mind, President Jefferson sent him to Philadelphia to meet with various scientists. According to one resource[1]:

> "In preparing for the Expedition, Lewis visited President Jefferson's scientific associates in Philadelphia for instruction in natural sciences, astronomical navigation and field medicine. He also was given a list of questions about their daily lives to ask the

---

[1] http://www.lewisandclark.org/LCTHF2/Expedition_History.html

American Indians that they would meet."

With this special training, Lewis would not only keep his men safe during the journey, but he could make sure that the American people would learn a lot about the Western part of the continent.

As a partner, Lewis chose his Army comrade William Clark, also a man accustomed to living in the outdoors and working hard. Lewis and Clark took care of training about four dozen men in a camp near St. Louis, Missouri, and then they set sail shortly afterward.

[3]
WHY DID LEWIS AND CLARK MAKE THEIR JOURNEY?

As we mentioned previously, this journey was very important because of:
- The Louisiana Purchase
- The chance to explore the territory west of the Mississippi
- Political reasons (laying claim to Oregon Territory).

Let's look at each of these reasons one by one.

The Louisiana Purchase. For some time, the French had controlled the Mississippi River. They had trade outposts on its banks, and they had a settlement in New Orleans. Napoleon, French ruler, sold the territory to Thomas Jefferson in 1803. By this time, Jefferson had already been making preparations for Lewis and Clark's trip. However, instead of simply exploring the Louisiana Territory (as was originally planned) they could now push all the way to the Pacific.

Jefferson and the rest of the American people wanted to know exactly what they had just bought. The price was so cheap (only $233 million in 2011 dollars, or less than 42 cents per acre). Can you imagine? So much land had been bought for so little money! Everyone was eager to find out what was there, and to see what was beyond.

The chance to explore the territory west of the Mississippi. Along with the Louisiana Purchase, there were also rumors from traders of beautiful animals that could be hunted and skinned.

Thomas Jefferson, himself a lover of nature, was also excited by the idea of discovering new and strange things. What would the land be like so far away from Washington? According to National Geographic magazine[2]:

> "When Thomas Jefferson dispatched Lewis and Clark to find a water route across North America and explore the uncharted West, he expected they'd encounter woolly mammoths, erupting volcanoes, and a mountain of pure salt."

Did you see that? The President of the United States thought that Lewis and Clark might see woolly mammoths and a mountain made out of salt on their journey! While it's hard to believe that people thought those things back then, it just helps us to understand how little everyone knew about these new territories. It would be an adventure to travel through them, and Lewis and Clark were eager to get started.

Political reasons (laying claim to Oregon Territory). Awe saw earlier, there were a lot of countries interested in these new lands. The French, the British, and the Spanish had all sent explorers to make discoveries west of the Mississippi and on the Pacific Coast. Up to this point, no one had really established any permanent forts of settlements in the Oregon/Washington area. Jefferson felt that, if the

---

[2] http://www.nationalgeographic.com/lewisandclark/

United States could travel from one coast to another and build a fort, then this would give them what's called a claim of "Discovery", which is kind of like a "finders, keepers" way of looking at things.

What's more, President Jefferson, like most Americans at the time, felt that it was the destiny of the United States to push further and further westward, until the country eventually covered all of the land from coast to coast. The first important step in doing this would be to explore the territory west of the Mississippi and claim it for the United States of America.

There were lots of important reasons for Americans to explore the territory west of the Mississippi, but these were the three that motivated President Jefferson to send Meriwether Lewis and William Clark on their adventure. But what actually happened on their journey? Let's find out.

[4]
What happened during Lewis and Clark's adventure?

On May 14, 1804, the journey began. Although there are a lot of interesting things to talk about, instead of looking at their journey chronologically (from start to finish) we're going to focus on some of the interesting things that they did and saw along the way.

Especially, we are going to focus on:
- The route they took
- The supplies they carried and the food they ate
- The adventures they had.

Let's begin learning about this amazing trip!

The route they took. As we saw earlier, Lewis and Clark thought that there might be some sort of a way to simply sail across the Western

United States, beginning with the Missouri River. They were hoping to sail up the Missouri River to its headwaters (where a river begins). They knew that the Columbia River, which flows westward to the Pacific Ocean, also had its headwaters in the same general area. Once they got to the beginning of the Missouri River, they were hoping that it would be possible to simply carry their boats for a short distance and then sail down the Columbia all the way to the Pacific.

In theory, they were right. But what they didn't know was that the headwaters of the Missouri and the headwaters of the Columbia lay on opposite sides of a HUGE mountain range- the Rocky Mountains. This mountain range is called the Continental Divide, because it acts like a huge wall separating one side of North America from the other. Lewis and Clark would end up leaving their boats on the east side and building new ones when they got to the western side.

One sad thing happened along the way, shortly after leaving. One man in their party, named Charles Floyd, died about three months after they left St Louis. It seems like his appendix exploded. Being so far away from any hospitals, there was nothing that anybody could do. The group buried him and continued on.

Things really got exciting after they had crossed the Rocky Mountains. They saw new animals (like the grizzly bear we mentioned in the introduction) and they had to ride with the current of the Columbia River, not against the current as they had done with the Missouri. At times, there were strong rapids, and the boats almost fell over. Have you ever been in a small raft or canoe on a rushing river? Did you fall into the water? Well, imagine Lewis and Clark doing the same thing, but without lifejackets or helmets. What's more, they also had to hold onto all of the supplies that we saw earlier, as well as the Lewis' giant dog (Seaman) and a small baby that was born along the way (named Jean Baptiste Charbonneau, he was the son of Sacagawea, a native American woman travelling with Lewis and Clark-we will talk about her more in a little bit).

Once they came to the end of the Columbia River, they finally saw the Pacific Ocean. Can you imagine how excited they were to finally see it? By that time, they had spent about one year and six months travelling. Do you think that they ever got tired along the way, and asked themselves if it was worth it? Do you think that they ever thought about going home?

We can imagine that at least some of the men, especially when it was cold, and they were hungry, thought about how nice it would have been to be in their warm beds back in the East. However, as difficult as things got, they always kept pushing forward.

Once they had reached the Pacific Ocean, the men spent the winter in a small fort that they had built and then began to head back in the spring. It wasn't easy going over the mountains, and the local tribe of Native Americans ended up sending some guides along to help the team get through the ten-foot-deep snow.

The team split into two just after crossing, in order to see a little bit more of the land (during this time, one of the men accidently shot Lewis, thinking that he was an elk! Thankfully, the bullet did no real damage). Then, they met back up and headed down the Missouri River towards St Louis.

All along the trip, they met up with fur trappers, men who lived by themselves and travelled from one place to another in the woods. They saw about eleven of these men during their two year and four-month voyage. As they were headed back to St Louis, some of the people that they met up with told them that everyone back home thought that they had died, and that they wouldn't be coming home. Can you imagine how surprised everyone must have been when the whole group came back? Over one thousand people, nearly everyone who lived in St Louis, ran outside to wave to the group as they passed by in their little boats. They shot their guns into the air and cheered. Lewis and Clark were heroes.

The supplies they carried and the food they ate. Realizing how important their journey was, the men didn't go unprepared. What kind of supplies did they bring? According to one source[3]:

> "The expedition was prepared with sufficient black powder and lead for their flintlock firearms, knives, blacksmithing supplies, and cartography equipment. They also carried flags, gift bundles, medicine and other items they would need for their journey. Much time went into ensuring a sufficient supply of these items."

The team didn't only have to prepare for all the dangers that they knew about, but also for the ones that might come as a surprise.

What's more, President Thomas Jefferson also had prepared several commemorative medals to be given out to the various Native American tribes along the way.

---

[3] http://en.wikipedia.org/wiki/Lewis_and_Clark_Expedition#Preparations

These medals would be like gifts for the tribes, but would also kind of make the United States government look like the stronger power. If the Native Americans accepted the medals (which had a message of friendship and peace) then (according to President Jefferson) it would be like their saying: 'Yes, we see that you are stringer and richer than us. We will do whatever you say and work together with you.' Do you agree? Do you think that President Jefferson should have expected all of the Native Americans to accept the authority of the United States so easily?

Along with food, guns, tool, and peace medals, Lewis and Clark had to bring their own boats with them. They had to be strong boats that would not flip over easily in rough river rapids, but that would also be light enough to carry around when the river was too shallow or too narrow. The men also had to be very strong to carry all of those supplies, right?

What kind of food did Lewis and Clark (along with their team) eat? Because they were always moving, there was no time to plant food. Also, they couldn't carry everything they wanted to (because they also had to carry tents, tools, and guns). So, what was the solution? The men had to get their food along the way.

They would hunt animals (like deer and antelope) whenever they could. They would eat the salmon that the Native Americans gave them, as well as roots and leaves from special plants. Sometimes, they didn't have enough food. Other times, when they saw a herd of buffalo, they would eat up to nine pounds of meat per day! Can you imagine that? That's like eating

36 hamburger patties every day! Why did they eat so much meat? Well, they wanted to get ready, just in case their food ran out again in the future.

Even though things got tough sometimes, the party never ran out of food, not even in the winter. No one starved to death, and everyone made it back to St Louis.

Now, let's talk about some of the exciting things that Lewis and Clark saw and did on their trip.

The adventures they had. Remember, Lewis and Clark were some of the first white Americans to see what was west of the Rocky Mountains. Although they didn't see any woolly mammoths or mountains made or salt (like

President Jefferson thought they might), they did eventually see about 300 new species of plants and animals. They even sent sample back to Washington DC. Among the samples was a live prairie dog, which no one east of the Mississippi had ever seen before!

They made contact with about two dozen Native American tribes. These relationships were important. Why? Well, many more white Americans would soon be travelling westward. It was important to know who they could trust and who could help them. The Native Americans were also happy to trade with the new people passing though. Not all of the Native Americans were helpful, however. For example, the Teton-wan Sioux tribe had a reputation for being very aggressive. When Lewis and Clark passed through, there was almost a big fight, but thankfully nothing ended up happening.

During their first winter, Lewis and Clark met a French-Canadian trapper named Toussaint Charbonneau. Although his wife Sacagawea was pregnant, she and her husband decided to travel with the group. She helped the Native American tribes along the way to communicate with Lewis and Clark. More than that, everyone felt a little better when they saw her holding her baby, because they realized that Lewis and

Clark weren't there to cause any problems. After all, they probably wouldn't have brought a young mother with them it they were looking for a fight. Along the way, Sacagawea even met up with a long-lost brother, who was a tribal chief. He helped Lewis and Clark a lot with their journey.

How were the different members of the group treated? Remember, there was a large group of white American men, but also one woman (Sacagawea) one African American slave (named York) and a French Canadian national (Toussaint Charbonneau). Yet, when it can time to make important decisions, everyone had an equal vote. This was very different from the way that things were done in the eastern United States. Back then, only rich white men could vote and decide on important decisions, even though everyone else had to deal with them. On this trip, everyone who was working hard could vote.

What do you think? Was it a good idea to let York, Toussaint Charbonneau, and Sacagawea be a part of the decision-making process along the way? Of course, it was! Unfortunately, over a hundred years would pass in the United States before every man and woman, no matter what color they were or what their background was, could vote in important political decisions. Lewis and Clark, however, all the way back in 1805, thought that everyone deserved to be listened to. Don't you agree?

Their trip was an exciting one. By the time they arrived back in St Louis on September 23, 1806, they had been where no one else had ever been, and they had learned things that would make the trip easier for those to follow.

[5]
What was it like to be a kid travelling with Lewis and Clark?

Most of the people who travelled with Lewis and Clark were men. They had been trained by the United States Army before volunteering or being chosen for this special job. The only young person was Sacagawea's son, born just before they crossed the Rocky Mountains. But even though there were no kids on the trail with them, can you imagine what it would have been like?

First, think about the walking. Although there were some exciting adventures, like discovering new plants and animals, and hunting buffalo, a lot of the time was just spent walking from one place to another. Can you feel the heavy backpack on your shoulders? Can you feel your sore feet take step after step along the way? Can you feel the sweat dripping down your forehead as you wonder when you will stop for a rest? It was hard to walk day after day, sometimes in the hot sun, with so much equipment. Eventually, the men would get horses, and each one would ride a horse and lead another that was loaded down with supplies. That made things a little easier.

What about the Native Americans? Would you have been scared to see them, or would you have tried to make friends? One of the Army privates who went with Lewis and Clark was named Private Pierre Cruzatte. He could speak the Omaha Native American language, and was also really good with sign language. He could even communicate with Native American tribes even though their languages were different. Would you have been like him?

What about the food? Remember, there were no stores or restaurants nearby, so if they wanted to eat, they had to hunt. Private John Collin was one of the main hunters in the group. How much did he have to capture each day? According to Lewis[4]:

---

[4] http://www.pbs.org/lewisandclark/inside/jcoll.html

"[I]t requires 4 deer, an Elk and a deer, or one buffaloe, to supply us plentifully for 24 hours."

Did you see how much food the group would eat each day? That means that men like Private John Collin had to do a lot of hunting, and a lot of butchering also. Could you have done that?

Think also about the time away from their family. The entire trip lasted about two and one half years (including the travel time to and from their home states). That means that these men didn't see their families for over 30 months! What's the longest you have gone without seeing your family? What about your friends? Do you think that the world had changed a lot by the time they came back?

Being on that trip would not have been easy for a kid. There would have been a lot of sacrifices, and a lot of dangers. But like the adults that went along, they also would have had a great adventure and would have been heroes to everyone back home!

[6] How did Lewis and Clark's journey end?

When the Discovery Corps completed their mission on September 23, 1806, they were greeted as heroes. The trip back hadn't been easy, but they had made it. They had completed their mission to travel all the way to the Pacific Ocean and to return. Although a lot of people thought that they had died along the way, it was a great celebration in St Louis when they finally returned.

Some of the Native Americans that they had met along the way went with them all the way back to St Louis and on to Washington DC.

The trail had been set for the thousands of white Americans who would ride the Oregon Trail and push westward across a very difficult and unforgiving terrain.

What Happened After Lewis and Clark Completed Their Journey?

On the way to Washington DC, where they would visit with the President and tell him all about their adventures, Lewis and Clark were treated like they had just returned from the moon. After all, put yourself fin the place of people living back then. Back when trains were only beginning to be developed, and 100 years before airplanes would fly, these two men had explored a completely new region on the United States. They came back with tales of huge grizzlies chasing them on the banks of rivers, massive herds of buffalo running on the open plains, and fierce Native Americans fighting with them over territory. They told of the vast Pacific Oceans and of the whales that beached themselves on its sands. They laughed about Lewis accidentally being shot (it was not serious) and talked about the snowcapped beauty of the Continental Divide.

In each and every city that they visited, they were the most important people there. They went to party after party, ceremony after ceremony. You can imagine that they probably told the same stories one hundred times each to all of the eager listeners.

Also, very importantly, they had established the claim of the United States to these lands. Within a short time, thousands of settlers would be moving west in search of gold and fortune.

What kind of rewards did the government give the soldiers who had travelled all the way to the Pacific[5]?

> "The men get double pay and 320 acres of land as rewards; the captains get 1,600 acres. Lewis is named governor of the Louisiana Territory; Clark is made Indian agent for the West and brigadier general of the territory's militia."

That's pretty exciting. They got huge pieces of land to build their house on a double their normal pay! Then, both the captains (Lewis and Clark) were given special government jobs.

But let's talk about later on down the road. What happened to all of these people? Although over 33 men were part of the Discovery Corps, along with some Native American guides and translators, we simply don't have time to talk about all of them. So, let's talk about some of the major characters in this

---

[5] http://www.pbs.org/lewisandclark/archive/1806.html

event, and see what happened to them later on, after they made history.
- Sacagawea
- Jean Baptiste Charbonneau
- York
- John Colter
- Meriwether Lewis
- William Clark

Sacagawea. Back at Mandan Village, Sacagawea, her husband, and her son say goodbye to Lewis and Clark. After staying a few more years away from Western Civilization, she moved with her family to be with William Clark in St Louis. She died of an unknown illness in 1812. In 1813, her former husband allowed Clark to adopt Sacagawea's son and daughter. He took care of them for the rest of their lives.

Jean Baptiste Charbonneau (son of Sacagawea). He was raised by Clark after his mother died. After he finished school, he spent a few years in Europe and then became a trapper and a hunter. Later, during the Mexican-American War, he served as a scout and helped to take supplies to US Army troops fighting in the field. After spending a few years in California during the Gold Rush, first looking for gold and then later operating a hotel, he died in an accident while travelling east on May 16, 1866.

York (Clark's slave). About ten years after the expedition ended, Clark granted York his freedom. He became a business man (working in shipping) and died sometime before 1832 of Cholera, a terrible disease.

John Colter. John Colter was one of the privates hired to go along with Lewis and Clark. He was a real rugged outdoorsman. At Fort Mandan, when Sacagawea and her family said goodbye to the captains, so did John Colter. With their permission, he returned to the wilderness to hunt beaver. During one trip up the Jefferson River in 1809, Colter was captured by Blackfoot Native Americans, who stripped him naked and killed his partner. They forced him to run for his life with a large group of warriors chasing after him. However, he was so athletic that he outrun all of them and escaped to a beaver lodge, where he spent the night. He later escaped to a fort, and decided to return to the civilized east. He died around 1812 of an illness called jaundice.

Meriwether Lewis. He was appointed Governor of the newly formed Louisiana Territory. When some questions arose as to how he had handled some of the government's money, he decided to travel to Washington DC in person to answer them. En route, on October 11,

1809, he died after being shot in the head. Most feel that it was a suicide, others think it was murder. Because he never had any children, his only descendants are through his sister.

William Clark. He served as Governor in Missouri for some time, and then later as Superintendent of Indian Affairs, appointed to that position by President James Monroe. His goal was to maintain peace with Native Americans, although he was forced, as part of his job, to relocate some as part of President Jackson's aggressive Indian Removal Act. In the meantime, he got married twice, had a total of eight children with his wives, and finally died himself on September 1, 1838 in St Louis, at his oldest son's house.

[7]
Conclusion

After having read through this report, what do you think? Was the expedition of the Discovery Corps, headed by Meriwether Lewis and William Clark an important moment in American history? Of course, it was! In fact, it was a real turning point for the growth of the United States. Let's see how.

It was the first step towards the formation of the Oregon Trail. Although Lewis and Clark didn't find an easy path to the Pacific, they did find out that it was possible to cross. They found two separate ways of climbing over the Rocky Mountains and, even more importantly, made detailed maps of each and every thing that they saw. These maps later helped the Mountain Men (trappers and prospectors) who would pave the way for the Oregon Trail.

Without the Oregon Trail, no one would have been able to settle the West.

It encouraged Americans to move west. How so? Well, the expedition of Lewis and Clark was like one big commercial for the Western United States. They spoke about wide open spaces and plenty of food and water. For people living in crowded cities back east, this was like talking about a paradise. It was a like a dream come true to hear about a land rich with natural resources and adventure. Within a few decades, thousands upon thousands of people would try to be like Lewis and Clark, and travel west.

It laid the foundation for future relations with Native American tribes. One of the goals of President Jefferson was to make sure that Native Americans would not present a problem as white Americans continued to press further and further into their lands. He decided that one of the best courses of action would be to send a lot of big guns along with Lewis and Clark, so that the Native Americans would be afraid of the superior firepower and technology of the United States Government.

Well, whether you think it was right or wrong, the trick worked. Lewis and Clark had little problems with Native Americans during their trip, and the good relationships they established would help future settlers travelling through those same lands.

Lewis and Clark were truly heroes. Although for many years no one really talked about all of their sacrifices and the things that they had accomplished, today they are among the most famous explorers in American history. Even when things were dangerous, they never thought about turning around and going home. They always tried their hardest to keep going, to keep moving forward, no matter what. Do you think that we can learn from their example? Of course, we can!

Although the entire United States has since been mapped out hundreds of times, there is always more to learn. There are always adventures to be had. Think about this: did Lewis and Clark really discover anything new? In reality, no, they didn't. The animals and plants that they saw had been around for thousands of years, and the people too. The Native Americans had been living on those lands for thousands of years too. What did Lewis and Clark really accomplish, then? They discovered something that was new to them and to the people they loved. Can you do the same?

Although you may never explore new lands (or even new planets) you can always learn something that is new to you! You can travel to a different country and get to know the people who live there. You can eat their food, learn their language, sing their songs, and dance their dances. You can have great new experiences, and then share them with the people you love. You can even write about your experiences like Lewis and Clark did, either in a journal or in a blog. Think about how many people would be excited to read about your adventures and your experiences. What other ways are there to have an adventure today?

Well, now that we have learned so much about the land on Earth, many scientists are looking deep into the ocean. Every trip, they see new plants and animals. Would like to do that? What kinds of dangers do you think there might be? Lewis and Clark had to fight grizzly bears and coyotes. They had to establish good relationships with Native Americans. What about in the ocean? Well, think about the huge sharks and the giant squids that may be dangerous. Think about the crushing pressure of the water when you are down so low. Think about how lonely it would be to spend weeks and months in the middle of the ocean, far away from you family. Sounds a lot like the expedition of Lewis and Clark doesn't it?

Also, other scientists are preparing to send probes to other planets, like Mars. Someday, they might even send people. Can you imagine the adventures that the people would have there? Maybe you can be one of the first! The trip alone would take months! Would you like to be one of the first space settlers and help to colonize a new planet? Do you think that there are any wild animals on Mars to worry about, or even any Native Martians? If Lewis and Clark were worried about other humans, who knows what Martian warriors would be like!

Lewis and Clark are two of the most famous explorers in American history. They were able to travel to new places and see new things. They brought back exciting reports, and they changed the history of the United States and the entire world. In our times, who knows what exciting discoveries we will see with our own eyes, and who knows how they will change the world. You can be a part of it!

But remember something important about Lewis and Clark: they were not the first, and they will not be the last. We humans love to learn! So why not try to be like them and find something new to do. If you do, you can be a real American adventurer, just like Lewis and Clark!

www.ingramcontent.com/pod-product-compliance
Lightning Source LLC
Chambersburg PA
CBHW052126070526
44586CB00016B/2110